SUSSEX
COUNTRY RECIPES

COMPILED BY
SARAH GOMAR

SUSSEX

Both Kent and Sussex are known as 'Gateway to England'. Today the term has romantic rural connotations. But ancient Britons saw it quite differently, for both counties were the popular gateway for successive waves of invaders. The Romans, Anglo-saxons and Normans used Sussex beaches and, once integrated, had a considerable influence on the local diet and how food was prepared.

Just inland from the coast are the Sussex Southdown hills, where the lush grass is grazed by the Southdown sheep which are exported all over the world. Sheep have roamed these Downs for over 5,000 years, and Sussex lamb is still a speciality. Rivers, such as Ouse and Arun criss-cross the county playing host to wild duck and a wide variety of fish including pike, chub, roach and perch.

Freshly caught sea fish, available from many of the Sussex ports is often sold from the actual fishing boats. Cod, plaice, lobster and crab are among the most popular.

Many traditional Sussex recipes have influenced British cooking. Suet pudding, the most renowned local dish, is to Sussex what Yorkshire 'pudding' is to Yorkshire. A basic suet pudding was filled with a savoury filling such as liver, lamb, or meatscraps, or a sweet filling such as raisins, apples or syrup.

'Duff' was the local term for dough. Swimmers, which were often served as 'elevenses', and were a great treat for children, get their name because they were served swimming in butter and sugar: pieces of suet dough were rolled out flat, dropped into boiling water and cooked for about twenty minutes. They were skimmed out, broken open with a fork (the old fashioned type only had three prongs) and served piping hot with a dollop of fresh farm butter and plenty of brown sugar in the centre.

Drip pudding was a plain boiled suet pudding, cut into thick slices and put into the dripping under the Sunday roast for about five minutes - good for making the meat go further round the family.

Lamb's tails and testicle pies ware made in the late Spring. A Rye sheep farmer's daughter can recall the skinning of the tails, but cannot remember exactly what happened to the other ingredient. This lady can also recall gathering samphire from the mud flats at Winchelsea, which was boiled and pickled and eaten like asparagus, with melted butter.

Rook pie was made by slitting the skin of the breast, folding it back and removing the best meat. The seasoned and floured breasts with the addition of sliced onion and herbs, were baked in a pie dish covered with a pastry lid. The pie was eaten hot or cold, when it would set into a delicious rich jelly.

Good restaurants and pubs are found in abundance in Sussex. The richness of the countryside, coastal resorts and places of interest are guaranteed to cater for all tastes.

RECIPES

SOUPS and BEGINNINGS

FISH

MEAT and GAME

SAVOURY PUDDINGS and PIES

VEGETABLE DISHES

CHUTNEYS and SAUCES

PUDDINGS

CAKES, BUNS and BISCUITS

CUCUMBER SOUP

Serves 4

2 good sized cucumbers
$1^{1/2}$ pints (900 ml/$3^{3/4}$ cups) vegetable stock
A little chopped sorrel and chervil
Salt and Pepper
1 tablespoon cream

Peel the cucumbers and chop into pieces.

Put on a plate and sprinkle with salt.

Leave for approximately 1 hour to draw out the water.

Drain and rinse.

Stew the cucumbers gently with the stock, herbs and seasoning for approximately 1 hour.

Stir in the cream before serving.

THE QUEEN'S FAVOURITE SOUP

Serves 6

This Victorian recipe for a creamy veal soup with barley, was given to a Sussex woman by one of the chefs in the Royal kitchen.

1/2 lb (225 g) pearl barley
3 pints (1.75 litres/$7^{1/2}$ cups) veal stock
1/2 pint (300 ml/$1^{1/4}$ cups) cream
Salt

Set the pearl barley in a stew pan with the veal stock.

Simmer very gently for $1^{1/2}$ hours.

Remove one third into another soup pot.

Rub the rest through a sieve and pour back into the barley.

Add the cream with a little salt.

Stir over the heat and serve hot.

TOMATO PATTIES

Serves 6

This is an old recipe recorded by Lady Elizabeth Shiffner, 1792-1861, who was married to Sir George Shiffner, 3rd Baronet, rector of St.Anne's Church of Lewes and Hamsey.

6 equal sized ripe tomatoes
1 tablespoon cream
Parsley chopped
2 egg yolks
Cayenne pepper
Salt

Wash the tomatoes and cut a small hole in the top of each.

Scoop out the inside carefully and pass through a sieve.

Add the cream, a little chopped parsley, a pinch of salt and cayenne pepper.

Blend in the yolks of egg.

Fill each tomato with the mixture.

Bake in a moderate oven for approximately 1/2 hour.

Serve up very hot with buttered toast.

Alternatively a small amount of any kind of potted meat can be added to the filling, or fried breadcrumbs can be sprinkled on top.

Oven: 350°F/180°C Gas Mark 4

SUSSEX FARMHOUSE PATE

Serves 6

This recipe will make about $2^{1/4}$ lbs (1 kg) of paté - at half shop prices.

1 lb (450 g) belly of pork
8 ozs (225 g) pig's liver
8 ozs (225 g) streaky or bacon pieces
4 ozs (100 g) brown breadcrumbs
1 medium onion
1 teaspoon of mixed herbs
Salt and black pepper

Remove all skin and bones from the pork, rind and bones from the bacon, and pipes from the liver.

Mince the meat twice with the onion, herbs, seasoning and breadcrumbs.

Put the mixture into a greased loaf tin.

Cover with foil, and place in a baking tin with water to come halfway up.

Bake in the centre of the oven for $1^{1/2}$ hours.

Do not strain off fat and juices.

Place a weight on top, and leave to get cold in the tin.

Turn out.

Oven: 300°F/150°C Gas Mark 2

HOT SUSSEX SMOKIES

Serves 4

1 lb (450 g) smoked haddock
2 oz (50 g) butter or margarine
2 oz (50 g) plain flour
1 pint (600 ml/2 1/2 cups) water
Salt and black pepper to taste
1 bay leaf
4 oz (100 g) Cheddar cheese
Few drops of tabasco sauce (optional)
Grated parmesan cheese (optional)

Poach the haddock in the water with the bay leaf.

Simmer for 10-15 minutes.

Reserve the fish stock.

Remove the skin and bones from the fish and flake.

Make a white sauce by melting butter, stirring in the flour to make a roux and gradually adding the reserved fish stock.

Remove from heat.

Add the seasoning.

Return to the heat.

Add the cheese, fish and tabasco sauce.

Continue to cook, stirring occasionally until smooth.

Spoon the mixture into four ramekin dishes.

Sprinkle the grated parmesan cheese over the top.

Place the dish in a roasting tin with 1/2 inch of water

Bake in the oven for 30 minutes.

Serve with thin slices of bread and butter.

Oven: 350°F/180°C Gas Mark 4

ARUNDEL MULLETS

Serves 4

This is traditionally made with grey mulet, an estuary fish which is rather difficult to obtain. It is common abroad, particularly around the Greek Islands. Red mullet, a round saltwater fish, is more easily obtainable, although it is unrelated to the grey mullet.

This dish dates from the 17th century, when it was served in soup plates. Bread was used to mop up the wine sauce. Still an excellent method to serve and eat Arundel mullets today.

4 mullets
1 pint (600 ml/2 1/2 cups) water or fish stock
1/2 oz (15 g) butter
2 medium onions, chopped
A little lemon juice
1/4 pint (150 ml/2/3 cup) red wine
2-3 anchovies
Bunch of sweet herbs, finely chopped
Salt and Pepper
Nutmeg

Prepare the mullets.

Simmer the fish gently in lightly salted water or stock for 10-15 minutes.

Lift out the fish, and reduce the liquid by half.

Melt the butter in a saucepan.

Add the onions and cook without browning.

Add the lemon juice, wine, reduced fish stock, anchovies, herbs, salt, pepper and nutmeg to taste.

Bring to the boil, return the mullets, and simmer very gently until done.

Serve with the sauce poured over the fish.

Shrimps may be used as an alternative to the anchovies.

CRAYFISH IN CREAM SAUCE

Serves 2

A freshwater crustacean, similar to a lobster, crayfish was once prolific in inland streams, although it is now rare. However, frozen tails are available.

Allow 12 crayfish tails for 2 persons
A tablespoon cream
A pinch of cayenne pepper
1/2 teaspoon sat
Anchovy essence
A little breadcrumbs or grated cheese

To prepare the crayfish drop into boiling water for a few minutes.

When they have turned pink, remove the shells.

Add the fish to traditional white sauce (see recipe) with cream, cayenne pepper, salt and anchovy essence.

Heat gently.

When hot, pour into scallop dishes.

Sprinkle with breadcrumbs or grated cheese.

Brown under the grill for a few minutes, before serving.

AMBERLEY TROUT

Serves 4

4 trout
A little fennel
1/4 pint (150 ml/2/3 cup) white wine
1 oz (25 g) cornflour
Salt and freshly ground black pepper
A little water

Season the trout with salt and freshly ground black pepper.

Place the fish in a buttered ovenproof dish.

Finely chop the fennel.

Sprinkle the fennel over the fish.

Pour over the white wine.

Cover with a lid or aluminium foil.

Bake for 25 minutes or until the fish is cooked.

Remove the trout and place on a serving dish.

Boil the liquid until it is reduced a little and thicken with the cornflour (mixed with a little cold water).

Adjust the seasoning to taste and pour over the fish.

Serve at once.

Oven: 350°F/180°C Gas Mark 4

PULBOROUGH EELS

Serves 3-4

Pulborough is on the river Arun with an abundance of freshwater fish. Another dish from Pulborough is 'steamed eel pudding'.

1 lb (450 g) skinned and boned eels
1 lb (450 g) suet pastry
2-3 oz (50-75 g) pickled pork
2 hard boiled eggs
1 small onion
1 tablespoon chopped parsley
Salt and pepper

Chop the pork and eggs.

Finely chop the onions.

Trim and cut the eels into small pieces.

Boil the eel trimmings with water for 10-15 minutes.

Grease a pudding basin and line with the suet pastry.

Leave enough pastry for a lid.

Put the eel pieces, pork, onion and eggs into the basin.

Sprinkle with parsley.

Add salt and pepper.

Pour the strained fish liquor over the ingredients.

Cover with the remaining suet pastry.

Pinch the edges together.

Cover with a cloth and tie securely.

Steam for 1 1/2 hours.

FRIED MACKEREL WITH ANCHOVY SAUCE

Serves 2

A rich and nourishing fish, still plentiful in the Sussex Waters. Mackerel is at its best absolutely fresh out of the sea and into the frying pan.

Rogation Day, 27th May, is marked by a religious service on the beach opposite the Old Ship Hotel, Brighton. The fishing boats are winched up on to the beach and the fisherman bring ashore their nets and mackerel catch for blessing.

2 medium mackerels
1 dessertspoon plain flour
Salt and pepper
2 oz (50 g) dripping

For the sauce:
1 oz (25 g) butter or margarine
1/2 teaspoon anchovy essence
1/2 teaspoon tarragon, freshly chopped
1/2 teaspoon parsley
1 tablespoon of vinegar

Wash and split the fish.

Remove the large centre bone, dry well and dust with seasoned flour.

Melt the dripping in a pan and when hot, put in the fish.

Fry over a medium heat for 5 minutes, turning half way through the cooking.

The roe may be cooked with the fish, if desired.

To make the sauce:

Melt the butter.

Stir in the anchovy essence, chopped tarragon, parsley and vinegar.

When very hot pour the sauce over the cooked fish and serve immediately.

TRADITIONAL EASTER SUNDAY LAMB

Serves 6

3 lb (1.5 kg) saddle of lamb
3/4 pint (450 ml/2 cups) red wine
2 tablespoons medium sherry
2 tablespoons brandy
6 sprigs rosemary
1 oz (25 g) dripping
2 tablespoons redcurrant jelly
Arrowroot

For the marinade:
1/2 carrot finely chopped
1 onion finely chopped
1 sprig parsley
3 fresh peppercorns
1 clove
1/2 teaspoon mace
2 tablespoons malt vinegar
A little water

Put all the ingredients for the marinade in a pan with a little water, enough just to cover the vegetables.

Bring to the boil and simmer for 30 minutes.

Leave to cool.

Stir in the wine, sherry and brandy.

Put in the lamb, covering well with marinade and leave for 12 hours.

Make a small incision in the lamb and fill with rosemary sprigs.

Spread the dripping over the marinated lamb and place in a roasting tin.

Cook for 2$^{1/2}$ hours.

Meanwhile boil the marinade quickly and reduce to 1 pint (600 ml/2$^{1/2}$ cups). Strain and stir in the redcurrant jelly.

Bring back to the boil and thicken with a little arrowroot (mixed previously with cold water).

Season to taste.

Serve the sauce with the lamb.

Oven: 350°F/180°C Gas Mark 4

SUSSEX STEW

Serves 4

A traditional favourite with the shepherds tending the famous Sussex Southdown sheep.

8 lamb chops (depending upon appetite)
1 large onion, chopped
2 tablespoons lentils
1 tablespoon brown sugar
1 pint (600 ml/2 1/2 cups) stock
1 lb (450 g) potatoes
Curry powder
Salt and pepper to taste

Cover the bottom of a casserole with the onions, lentils and brown sugar mixed with salt and pepper.

Trim the chops, and press each one into the curry powder.

Place on top of the onion mixture.

Peel the potatoes, and cut into round slices

Add the stock.

Cover with the potato slices.

Cover the casserole and cook in the oven for 2 1/2 hours.

Remove the lid to brown the potatoes for the last 20 minutes.

Oven: 350°F/180°C Gas Mark 4

SUSSEX WHEEL LAMB PIE

Serves 4

1 lb (450 g) sliced lamb, cooked
8 oz (225 g) tin of asparagus
1 lb (450 g) mashed potato
1 onion, chopped
1 tablespoon mint, chopped
1/2 pint (300 ml/1 1/4 cups) stock
Salt and pepper to taste

Gently fry the onion until lightly brown.

Put the lamb slices in an oven dish.

Cover with the onion, stock and chopped mint.

Add salt and pepper to taste.

Place in the oven and bring to a slow simmer.

Cook the potatoes while the meat is warming in the oven.

Smooth the mashed potato over te meat.

Make eight grooves like the spokes of a wheel radiating from the centre.

Return the dish to the oven to brown the potato.

Lay eight asparagus tips along the grooves to form the wheel.

Return the dish to the oven for a few minutes to heat the asparagus through before serving.

Oven: 350°F/180°C Gas Mark 4

ROAST LAMB SUSSEX STYLE

Serves 4-6

In England there are traditional methods of cutting meat which vary from region to region.

Sussex butchers remove the large bladebone from a shoulder of lamb giving it a better shape and making it easier to carve once cooked. The removal of the bladebone leaves a large pocket which is ideal for stuffing. This is a typical stuffing which is delicious and has been used for stuffing lamb since the 19th century.

A shoulder of lamb - about 4 lbs (1.75 kg)
1 lb (450 g) mushrooms
1 1/2 oz (40 g) butter
Salt
Cayenne pepper
1/2 teaspoon grated nutmeg

Wash, dry and slice the mushrooms.

Melt the butter in a pan, add the mushrooms and cook gently.

Add a little salt, cayenne pepper and the nutmeg.

Fill the shoulder blade pocket with the mushrooms.

Pin together with skewers.

Spread the 1 1/2 oz butter on the lamb.

Cover with foil and roast in a moderate oven for 20 minutes per lb plus 20 minutes extra.

No need to baste.

If you wish to have crispy meat open the foil for the last 20-30 minutes.

Oven: 350°F/180°C Gas Mark 4

SHEEP'S TROTTERS AND CUCUMBER

Serves 6-8

An old recipe from Aldwick in West Sussex.

2 'gangs' of sheep's trotters - 8
1 large cucumber
1 tablespoon salt
2 tablespoons vinegar
2 oz (50 g) butter
1 teaspoon powdered ginger
2-3 tablespoons parsley chopped
2 or 3 onions chopped
A pinch of grated nutmeg
A pinch of cayenne pepper
1 clove garlic (optional)
2 tablespoons white sauce
3 egg yolks
1/4 pint (150 ml/2/3 cup) milk or cream
1 dessertspoon lemon juice

Boil the sheep's trotters until tender.

Let them get cold, and divide into three pieces.

Peel the cucumber, dice and put into a basin with salt and vinegar.

Let it lie for an hour.

Drain and put into the pan with butter, powdered ginger, chopped parsley, chopped onion, nutmeg, cayenne pepper and garlic.

Simmer ingredients together for 1 1/2 hours.

Pour off the butter and add 2 tablespoons of white sauce or broth thickened with flour.

Simmer for a few more minutes.

Add beaten egg yolks and milk or cream.

Stir until thickened but do not boil.

Add lemon juice

Meanwhile boil trotters again and when hot place in a serving dish.

Pour over the sauce and serve.

STUFFED LAMB CUTLETS

Serves 6

6 good sized lamb cutlets

For the stuffing:
1 large onion, chopped
4 oz (100 g) breadcrumbs
4 oz (100 g) minced ham
1 egg beaten
A little milk
2½ oz (65 g) suet
2 teaspoons chopped parsley
1/4 teaspoon of thyme and marjoram
Salt and pepper

Prepare the chops.

Cut a slit near the bone to make a pocket.

Mix the onion, breadcrumbs, ham, suet, herbs and seasoning with beaten egg and a little milk to bind it together.

Stuff each chop and spread any remaining stuffing over the top of the meat.

Loosely wrap individual chops in foil.

Bake in a moderate oven for 45 minutes.

Oven: 375°F/190°C Gas Mark 5

BEEF STEW

Serves 6

A traditional recipe that differs little from a modern stew.

2 lb (900 g) braising steak
1 onion
2 carrots
4 oz (100 g) mushrooms (optional)
1/2 pint (300 ml/1 1/4 cups) stock
1 glass red wine
Bouquet garni
Salt and pepper

Wash and dice the meat.

Peel and slice the onion, carrots and mushrooms.

Place the meat and vegetables in a oven-proof dish.

Add seasoning and herbs.

Pour the wine into the stock and add.

Cover with a lid and cook in the oven for at least 2 hours or until the meat is tender.

Oven: 350°F/180°C Gas Mark 4

CHIDDINGLY HOT-POT

Serves 4

An all-in-one family casserole which originates from the village of Chiddingly, about five miles from Ringmer.

1 lb (450 g) stewing steak
A little allspice
Seasoned flour
1 oz (25 g) dripping
4 ozs (100 g) chopped celery
4 ozs (100 g) chopped onions or shallots
1 lb (450 g) sliced potatoes
8 ozs (225 g) olives, stoned and chopped
1 teaspoon tarragon
Vinegar
1/2 oz (15 g) melted butter
1/2 pint (300 ml/1 1/4 cups) stock
Salt and pepper to taste

Cut the meat into cubes and dust with the seasoned flour.

Brown the meat in the dripping.

Remove from the pan and fry the celery, olives and onions lightly.

Put a layer of onions, olives and celery in a casserole dish.

Sprinkle with allspice, salt and pepper.

Cover with a layer of meat and a thin layer of potatoes.

Repeat these layers, seasoning and adding the vinegar.

Finish with a layer of potatoes and brush with melted butter.

Add the stock to come just below the potatoes.

Cover with a lid and cook in the oven for 1 1/2 hours.

Remove the lid and continue cooking to brown the potatoes for another hour.

Oven: 325°F/160°C Gas Mark 3 for 2 1/2 hours.

SIRLOIN OF BEEF, THE FILLET-HASH'D

This recipe is taken from The Cooks Paradise 1759 by William Verral. William Verral succeeded his father as second Master of the White Hart and became a pioneer of English food, as we know it today.

The White Hart Inn (now Hotel) is situated in the busy town centre of Lewes, the county town of Sussex, only 12 miles from the coast. It was originally a 14th century country mansion, and in the early 18th century became a coaching Inn of some repute under the Master Richard Verral, and the meeting place for official functions and parliamentary election parties. Among its most noted historic meetings was that of the 'Headstrong Club' founded in 1768 by Thomas Paine, Champion of the Rights of Man and one of the founders of American Independence. A plaque outside the hotel reads:

'Thomas Paine 1737-1809 here expounded revolutionary politics. This Inn is regarded as a cradle of American Independence, which he helped to found with pen and sword'.

Trim your beef to look decent and put it into a marinade the day before, wrap it up in paper to roast it; take out the inside fillet and slice it very thin, take care of your gravy and put your meat into a stew pan with it as much cullis* as is necessary to well fill the part where the meat was taken out with some flouring in the dish, season with only pepper, salt, a shallot or two and minced parsley, make it thorough boiling hot, add the juice of a lemon and serve it up what we call the wrong side uppermost.

*cullis - strong broth of meat, boiled and strained.

SUSSEX FARMHOUSE LIVER

Serves 4

4 slices calves or pigs liver
8 rashers streaky bacon
4 tablespoons breadcrumbs
2 tomatoes, sliced
4 oz (100 g) mushrooms, sliced
1 onion
Parsley (chopped)
Mixed herbs
Salt and pepper
1 egg (beaten)
Worcester sauce
Gravy if desired

Chop the onion.

Mix with the chopped parsley, herbs, breadcrumbs, seasoning and beaten egg.

Form four balls of this mixture, and place one on each slice of the liver.

Wrap each slice of liver securely in the streaky bacon.

Place the tomatoes and mushrooms in an ovenproof dish.

Put the liver on top.

Add a little Worcester sauce.

Cover with foil and cook in the oven for 30 to 40 minutes.

Halfway through the cooking a little gravy may be added if desired.

Oven: 350°F/180°C Gas Mark 4

TRIPE ROMAINE

Makes 5-6

2 lb (900 g) tripe
2 large onions
3 leeks
1 small head celery
6 tomatoes
2 oz (50 g) dripping
1 glass dry cider
Salt and pepper
2 oz (50 g) grated cheese

Cut the tripe into lengths.

Boil in salted water until tender.

Slice the onion, leek and celery and fry in dripping until golden brown.

Strain the tripe.

Add the vegetables and the sliced tomatoes.

Add the cider.

Put the ingredients in an ovenproof dish.

Cook in a moderately hot oven for 15 minutes.

Remove from the oven.

Sprinkle grated cheese over top and return to the oven to brown.

Oven: 375°F/190°C   Gas Mark 5

ISFIELD VICARAGE HOG'S PUDDING

A pork sausage savoury from Isfield - a village about three miles from Lewes, the county town of Sussex.

This dish is said to have originated from the Isfield Vicarage School around 1860. When one of the Vicar's pigs was killed, the six private pupils were served with a second course that they called 'Hog's Puddings'. A pupil reported 'They were generally served cold, done up like sausage in skins, in clusters of three or more, and were more of a sweetmeat than a savoury'. Hog's Pudding is usually the size of an egg and irregular in shape. Today it is generally eaten as either a hot or cold savoury.

1 lb (450 g) pork (flank)
A little baking powder
1½ oz (40 g) flour
A little allspice
1 lb (450 g) currants
Some sausage skins (from the butchers)
1 lb (450) lard

Cut the meat into small pieces and put on to boil gently for about 1 hour.

Mix the flour and baking powder with the meat, currants and spice and rub in the lard.

Fill the sausages skins and tie up in bunches.

Prick the sausages with a fork and drop into boiling water.

Simmer for 1½ hours.

Take out and hang up to dry.

The sausages will snap easily when broken in two.

SUSSEX BRAWN

This is a very old Sussex recipe - dating from the 18th century.

Pig's head, feet and tongue
6 oz (175 g) sugar
$1^{1/2}$ oz (40 g) salt petre
6 oz (175 g) salt
1/4 pint (150 ml/2/3 cup) vinegar
1 onion
2 carrots
2 celery sticks
A little mixed spice

Take the pigs head and cut off the ears.

Clean the head well and cut in half.

Clean the feet and ears.

Prepare the mixture of sugar, salt petre and rub into the feet and ears.

Let them remain for a few hours and rub in the salt.

After 12 hours pour over the vinegar.

Leave for a week turning the pieces daily.

Drain the pieces and wash.

Cook gently until all the bones can be easily removed.

Flatten the halves of the head - keeping them in shape as much as possible.

Sprinkle with a little mixed spice.

Place the ears, feet and tongue in the centre and roll into shape.

Tie round tightly and fasten in a cloth.

Cover with water.

Add chopped onion and celery and boil for 4 hours.

Let the roll cool in the liquor.

Drain off and press between weights for one or two days.

Take off the cloth then and it is ready for the table

PORK IN CIDER WITH CHEESE TOPPING

Serves 2-3

8 oz (225 g) diced pork (cooked)
1 large onion
1 clove garlic
1pint (600 ml/2$^{1/2}$ cups) cider
1 oz (25 g) cornflour
Salt and pepper
2 oz (50 g) grated cheese

Chop the onion and crush the garlic.

Put in a pan and fry gently with the diced pork for approximately 15 minutes.

Add the cider.

Season lightly.

Thicken with a little cornflour (mixed with cold water).

Sprinkle with grated cheese and serve.

BROILED PARTRIDGE

Serves 2-3

1 whole young partridge
1 dessertspoon rice
1 onion
1 pint (600 ml/2½ cups) mutton or veal broth
Salt to taste

Chop the onion into fine pieces.

Split the partridge down the back and clean with a soft cloth inside and out.

Put in a pan with the broth, rice, onion and a little salt.

Stew until tender.

Serve in a deep dish.

BROILED PARTRIDGE WITH MUSHROOM SAUCE

Serves 2-3

1 whole young partridge
Sufficient water to cover
1 oz (25 g) butter
Salt and cayenne pepper

For the sauce:
2 oz (25 g) butter
2 tablespoons flour
A little water
Salt and cayenne pepper
Mushroom catsup (ketchup) - see recipe

Boil the partridge in the water until tender.

When cooked, sprinkle with salt and cayenne pepper and rub in fresh butter.

To make the sauce:

Melt the butter in a pan.

Add flour, water and mix to a smooth consistency.

Add cayenne pepper and salt and a little mushroom catsup.

Pour the sauce over the partridge and serve.

ROAST WILD DUCK WITH APRICOTS

Serves 6

This stuffing and method could alternatively be used for roast chicken.

4 lb (1.75 kg) duck
Salt and pepper
5 oz (150 g) dried apricots
1 lemon

Soak the apricots for 6-8 hours.

Drain the apricots and retain the liquid.

Prepare the duck and cut 4 oz (100 g) of the apricots into halves.

Grate the lemon thinly and squeeze out the juice.

Mix the apricots, lemon rind and juice together.

Use the mixture to stuff the bird.

Put into a roasting dish and baste with 4 tablespoons of reserved apricot liquid.

Roast the duck for 2 hours until brown.

Baste during cooking.

Serve garnished with the remainder of the whole apricots.

Oven: 350°F/180°C Gas Mark 4

NORMAN PIE

Serves 4

1 lb (450 g) cooked chicken or rabbit
2 oz (50 g) macaroni
2 oz (50 g) parmesan cheese
1 shallot, finely chopped
Salt and pepper
7 fl oz (200 ml/3/4 cup) double cream
Vermicelli

Boil the meat and when cooked cut as thinly as possible.

Cook the macaroni until tender.

Mix the parmesan cheese, shallot, pepper and salt with the cream.

Add macaroni and meat.

Put into a dish,sprinkle with vermicelli and serve hot.

HAM AND SHERRY

Serves 4-6

Traditionally recommended for breakfast on Saturday, as quite a way to start the weekend.

1 lb (450 g) sliced ham
1 1/2 oz (40 g) butter
1 tablespoon of meat jelly
Worcester sauce
1/2 teaspoon pepper
1/2 glass sherry

Fry the slices of ham in butter and take out of the pan.

Add the meat jelly, a dash of Worcester sauce, pepper and sherry.

Let it all boil up in the pan.

Pour over the ham and serve hot.

HARD DUMPLINGS

It is traditionally said that only a Sussex woman can make hard dumplings or puddings successfully.
When cooked these were often cut into 1 inch thick slices and placed for 20-30 minutes in the dripping pan under the meat roasting in front of the fire. Alternatively they would be used with a stew.

8 oz (225 g) plain flour
A pinch of sat
Water to mix

Make a light dough with the flour, pinch of salt and sufficient water to mix.

Shape into balls.

Dust with flour and boil them for nearly an hour.

TRADITIONAL SAVOURY SUET PASTRY OR SUET CRUST

This is a basic suet pasty used in traditional savoury puddings.

8 oz (225 g) plain flour
4 oz (100 g) suet shredded
A little cold water

Mix together the flour and shredded suet.

Add a little cold water until a thick consistency is achieved.

Roll out on a floured surface and use as required.

SUSSEX BLANKET PUDDING

Serves 4

Suet pudding is to Sussex what Yorkshire pudding is to Yorkshire. On Sussex farms at the turn of the century, a blanket pudding was usually served at least once a week - twice if money was short. The fillings can be either sweet or savoury, and a variety are given below.

12 ozs (350 g) plain flour
6 ozs (175 g) suet
2 eggs (beaten)
8 ozs (225 g) breadcrumbs
Salt and pepper to taste
A little milk to mix

Mix the flour, suet, breadcrumbs and seasoning together.

Fold in the eggs.

Mix to a light dough with the milk.

Roll out into a oblong shape.

Spread the pastry with one of the fillings (see below).

Damp the edges of the pastry, and fold into a parcel, pressing the edges firmly together.

Tie the pudding in a floured cloth.

Boil for 2 hours.

Fillings (Savoury):

Liver and bacon minced with parsley and onion.

Sausage meat.

Any scraps of meat, minced with onions.

Fillings (Sweet):

Jam.

Golden syrup.

Mincemeat.

Chopped cooking apples, mixed with a little butter and 2 tablespoons orange marmalade.

Currants, raisins and chopped peel mixed with 2 tablespoons sugar.

HAROLD'S RYE FISH PUDDING

Serves 4

The favourite recipe of an old Rye fisherman.

1 lb (450 g) suet pastry
1½ lbs (675 g) white fish
1 oz (25 g) butter
Salt and pepper to taste

Remove the skin and bones from the fish.

Cut into 1 inch chunks.

Line a 2 pt greased pudding basin with three quarters of the suet pastry.

Put the fish into the basin, seasoning each layer.

Cut the butter into small pieces and dot over the top.

Cover with the remaining pastry rolled out as a lid.

Cover the basin with foil or greaseproof paper and a pudding cloth.

Steam for 2 hours.

ASHDOWN PARTRIDGE PUDDING

Partridge or pigeon pudding was once popular in the Ashdown forest area and special basins to cook the pudding were made in Sussex. They were wide and fluted and without a rim. The rim was evidently unnecessary as the whole basin was tied in a cloth, rather than just the top, as is customary nowadays.

2 partridges (boilers)
4 oz (100 g) rump steak
4 oz (100 g) mushrooms
1 tablespoon chopped fresh parsley or a pinch of dried parsley
Salt and pepper
A pinch of mixed herbs
1 glass of claret or red wine
1 pint (600 ml/2$^{1/2}$ cups) stock

For the suet crust pastry:
1/2 lb (225 g) suet
1 lb (450 g) plain flour
A little water

Mix together the suet, plain flour and water for the suet crust.

Grease a pudding basin and line with the suet crust.

Keep enough suet pastry for the lid of the pudding.

Thinly slice the steak and lay at the bottom of the pudding.

Cut the partridges into joints and add to the meat.

Chop the mushrooms.

Add the mushrooms and the herbs to the meat.

Season with salt and pepper.

Pour over the claret or wine and the stock.

Make a lid with the remaining suet pastry, pinching the edges together.

Cover the pudding with a cloth.

Stand in a saucepan of water and boil for 3 hours. Do not allow to boil dry.

SUSSEX CHICKEN PUDDING

Serves 2

Suet crust (made with 8 oz (225 g) flour and 4 oz (100 g) suet)
2 chicken joints
4 oz (100 g) chopped ham)
2 carrots
2 sticks celery
1/2 teaspoon tarragon
Salt and pepper

Prepare the suet crust (see recipe)

Line the basin.

Keep enough for a lid.

Chop the carrots and celery finely.

Put the chicken joints, vegetables and herbs into a basin.

Season with salt and pepper.

Cover with the remaining suet crust.

Seal the edges.

Cover with a cloth and tie securely.

Steam for 2-2 1/2 hours.

HEART PUDDING

Serves 2

Suet crust
(made with 8 oz (225 g) flour and 4 oz (100 g) suet)
1 calf's heart
2 oz (50 g) breadcrumbs
1 tablespoon freshly chopped parsley
1 tablespoon freshly chopped thyme
Salt and pepper

Prepare the suet crust (see recipe).

Clean the heart well.

Mix the breadcrumbs, herbs and seasoning.

Moisten with a little milk or water.

Put the mixture in the heart cavities and sew together with thread.

Roll out the suet crust.

Place the prepared heart in the centre.

Roll out the pasty firmly round, dampen the edges and press together.

Put in a cloth and tie securely.

Boil for 2-2½ hours.

Note: Remove the thread before serving.

SUSSEX RABBIT & PIGEON PUDDING

Makes 5-6 portions

1 rabbit, jointed
2 woodpigeon's breasts
1/2 lb (225 g) pickled pork, diced
1 tablespoon flour
1 teaspoon salt
1/4 teaspoon pepper

For the suet crust:
8 oz (225 g) flour
4 oz (100 g) shredded suet
A little cold water to mix

Put the liver and kidney of the rabbit aside (which can later be stewed).

Mix the flour, salt and pepper together.

Slice the pigeon breast.

Coat the rabbit and pigeon breasts with the flour mixture.

Line a basin with the suet crust, leaving enough to make a lid.

Put in the rabbit, pigeon and diced pork, closely packed into the basin.

Put on the pasty lid.

Dampen the edges and press together to seal.

Cover with a cloth.

Steam for at least 2 1/2 hours.

SUSSEX BACON PUDDING

Serves 2

A favourite in Sussex for many generations.

4 oz (100 g) flour)
2 oz (50 g) suet
1 onion, finely chopped
1 teaspoon mixed herbs
4 rashers of bacon - diced
1 egg
1-2 tablespoons milk

Mix the flour and suet together.

Heat a little oil in a pan and fry the onion.

Add the bacon.

When cooked remove and add to the suet mixture.

Stir in the herbs, egg and milk to give a 'dropping' consistency.

Pour into a greased basin.

Cover with a cloth and steam for 1½ hours.

SUSSEX BACON ROLY POLY

Serves 4

When traditionally served, the bacon rashers were laid across the pastry so that the fat and lean were evenly shared.

8 oz (225 g) self-raising flour
4 oz (100 g) chopped suet
12 oz (350 g) bacon, chopped
1 onion, sliced
2 dessertspoons freshly chopped sage or 2 teaspoons dried sage
Salt and pepper

Sift the flour with a little salt.

Add the suet. Add a little water and mix to a stiff consistency.

Roll out thinly on a floured surface.

Place the bacon, onion and sage on the prepared pastry.

Season with salt and pepper;

Roll into a long roll.

Wrap in greaseproof paper and then in a cloth.

Tie ends securely.

Put in boiling water and simmer for 2-2$^{1/2}$ hours.

SUSSEX MOCK PORK PIE

Shortcrust pastry
2/3 ozs (50-75 g) bacon for each person
1 egg for each person
1/2 small teaspoonful of mixed herbs
Pepper and salt to taste

Line a shallow pie dish with shortcrust pastry.

Arrange the chopped bacon in it.

Sprinkle with the herbs.

Break in carefully one egg for each person.

Add pepper and salt to taste.

Cover with pastry and bake until pastry is cooked.

Serve hot or cold.

Oven: 375°F/190°C Gas Mark 5

SUSSEX SAVOURY PIE

Serves 4

This dish is a good stand-by; it tastes just as good re-heated.

8 ozs (225 g) shortcrust pastry
4 rashers bacon
Chopped onion
Salt and pepper
2 eggs
Mashed potato
Butter and milk
Little dried sage

Line a pie-dish with the pastry. Keep enough for a lid.

Put in 2 rashers of bacon.

Sprinkle with sage and a little chopped onion.

Cover with mashed potato (well seasoned and mixed with butter and milk).

Pour on well beaten eggs, seasoned with salt and pepper.

Add 2 rashers and cover with the remaining pastry.

Cook for about 30 minutes.

Oven: 375°F/190°C Gas Mark 5

SUSSEX CHURDLES

Serves 4

Traditional liver, bacon and mushroom pasties which are shaped like a Bishop's hat.

8 oz (225 g) shortcrust pastry
4 oz (100 g) liver
4 oz (100 g) bacon
1 oz (25 g) mushrooms
1 onion
1 apple
1 dessertspoon parsley, chopped
1 tablespoon breadcrumbs
1 tablespoon grated cheese
Salt and pepper to taste
1 oz (25 g) cooking fat

Mince the liver and bacon.

Finely chop the onion, mushrooms and apple.

Add to the meat.

Add the parsley and seasoning to taste.

Mix together.

Roll out the pastry.

Using an upturned saucer as a guide, cut out rounds.

Pile the mixture into the middle of each round.

Dampen the edges of the pastry.

Pull up each round, but leave the centre open, to form the bishop's hat.

Press the edges of the pastry together.

Mix together the cheese and breadcrumbs, and sprinkle on the top of each pasty.

Bake for 20 minutes until golden brown.

Oven: 425°F/3220°C Gas Mark 7

STEWED NETTLES

Serves 2-3

Nettles were formerly used as a vegetable in England, and often included in soups and used for making beer.

A bunch of young nettles, about 1 lb (450 g)
A pinch of salt and pepper
1 oz (25 g) butter
1 tablespoon cream

Wash the nettles.

Bring sufficient water to cover the nettles in a pan to the boil.

Add the nettles and cook for 5-10 minutes.

Strain and mash.

Add the butter, cream and seasoning.

Re-heat and serve.

CREAMED PARSNIP OR SWEDE

A more interesting way of serving parsnips and swede.

Peel and cut the vegetables in cubes.

Cook in boiling salted water for approximately 15 minutes or until tender.

Note: Parsnips should be added to boiling water, swedes are put in cold water and brought to the boil.

Drain the vegetables and purée with a little cream, and season to taste.

BRAISED CELERY WITH CREAM SAUCE

Serves 6

The cream sauce with this dish is also excellent with baked or grilled fish.

2 large heads of celery
2 oz (50 g) butter or margarine
Salt and pepper

For the cream sauce:
1 pint (600 ml/2½ cups) double cream
3 oz (75 g) butter or margarine
Salt and pepper

Discard the coarse outer stalks but retain some of the green celery tops.

Chop the tops finely.

Wash, prepare and cut the celery into 3 pieces.

Put into a fireproof dish.

Cut the fat into small pieces and dot on the top.

Season with salt and pepper.

Cover the dish with a lid or foil.

Cook in the oven for 40 minutes.

To make the cream sauce:

Bring the cream to the boil.

Simmer gently until it is slightly reduced.

Add the butter or margarine and stir until melted

Season with salt and pepper.

Stir in the chopped celery tops into the sauce.

Pour over the braised celery.

Oven: 375°F/190°C Gas Mark 5

BAKED POTATOES WITH HERBY-CHEESE FILLING

Serves 4

4 potatoes (for baking)
4 oz (100 g) cream cheese
1 egg beaten
2 oz (50 g) onion chopped
1 tablespoon parsley (freshly chopped)
1 tablespoon chives (chopped)
Salt and pepper

Wash and prick the potatoes.

Bake in the oven until cooked for approximately 1-1½ hours.

Cut the potatoes in half.

Scoop out a dessertspoon of potato from each and mix with the cheese, onion, egg and herbs.

Season to taste.

Pile the mixture into the potatoes.

Put under the grill for 5-10 minutes.

Serve very hot.

Oven: 425°F/220°C Gas Mark 7

POTATO JANE

Serves 4

Potatoes are very much part of the stanle English diet but in war-times when meat was rationed and scarce they were often the mainstay, providing nourishing meals rich in vitamin C. Delicious potato dishes are still very much a favourite.

1$^{1/2}$ lb (675 g) potatoes
3 oz (75 g) grated cheese
2 oz (50 g) breadcrumbs
1 leek
Salt and pepper
1/2 pint (300 ml/1$^{1/4}$ cups) milk

Peel and thinly slice the potatoes.

Chop the leek.

Mix potatoes and leeks together.

Grease an ovenproof dish.

Mix the breadcrumbs and cheese together.

Season with salt and pepper.

Cover the bottom of the dish with a layer of potato and leek and then a layer of cheese and breadcrumbs.

Continue the layers finishing with a cheese layer.

Pour over the milk.

Bake in a moderate oven until the potatoes are soft (approximately 45 minutes).

Oven: 350°F/180°C Gas Mark 4.

VEGETABLE PIE

Serves 4

Other seasonal or favourable vegetables can be used as a variation.

8 oz (225 g) shortcrust pastry
1 onion
2 carrots
1 small turnip
1 artichoke
2-3 cauliflower florets
2 oz (50 g) butter
1 teaspoon freshly chopped thyme
1 teaspoon freshly chopped marjoram
1 tablespoon freshly chopped parsley
2 tablespoons tomato purée
Salt and pepper
Beaten egg to glaze

Peel and dice the onion, carrots, turnip and artichoke;

Melt the butter in a pan and gently cook all the vegetables.

Add the herbs, tomato purée and seasoning.

Mix together well.

Line an ovenproof dish with the pastry.

Fill with the vegetable mixture, packing it down firmly.

Cover with a pastry lid and brush with the beaten egg.

Prick the pastry and bake in the oven for approximately 40 minutes or until golden brown.

Oven: 200°C/400°F Gas Mark 6

ARTICHOKE PIE

Serves 4

8 oz (225 g) shortcrust pastry
1 lb (450 g) Jerusalem artichokes
1 onion
1 teaspoon mixed herbs
1 oz (25 g) butter (cut into small pieces)
Salt and pepper to taste
1/2 lb (225 g) potatoes (butter, milk, sat and pepper for mashing)

Prepare the pastry.

Line a greased dish with the pastry.

Peel, de-knobble and slice the artichokes.

(Keep in cold water to prevent discolouration)

Peel and slice the onion.

Place the vegetables and herbs in the pie.

Season and dot with butter.

Cover with foil and cook in the oven for 30-35 minutes.

Meanwhile, peel, slice and cook the potatoes in boiling water for 20 minutes or until tender.

Drain and mash.

Add a little butter and milk and mix well.

Season with salt and pepper.

Spread the potatoes on top of the vegetables.

Return to the oven for 10 minutes to brown.

Oven: 400°F/200°C Gas Mark 6

TOMATO PIE

Serves 4

8 oz (225 g) shortcrust pastry
1 onion
1 oz (25 g) dripping or butter
1 lb (450 g) tomatoes
2 oz (50 g) grated cheese
4 oz (100 g) breadcrumbs
Seasoning

Roll out the pasty on a floured surface.

Lien a pie dish with the pastry.

Chop the tomatoes.

Mix half the breadcrumbs with half the cheese.

Add the tomatoes.

Place in a dish pie with the thinly sliced onion.

Season well.

Put the remaining cheese and breadcrumbs on top of the mixture.

Dot the top with butter or dripping.

Bake for 30 minutes in a moderate oven.

Oven: 400°F/200°C Gas Mark 6

HOT TOMATO CHUTNEY Makes 5-6 lbs (2.75 kg)

4 lb (1.75 kg) ripe tomatoes
1 pt (600ml/2 1/2 cups) vinegar
1/2 lb (225 g) green ginger
1 lb (450 g) raisins
1 oz (25 g) red chillies
1 1/2 lb (675 g) sugar
2 oz (50 g) salt
1 clove of garlic - according to taste

Chop the tomatoes.

Put into a pan and boil until the liquid is reduced by half.

Add the vinegar.

Mix together the raisins, ginger and chillies.

Add the tomato mixture.

Stir in the sugar, salt and ground garlic.

Boil until the liquid thickens.

Cool and bottle in 1 lb jars.

SUSSEX CHUTNEY

Makes about 6 lbs (2.75 kg)

2 cloves garlic
2 lbs (900 g) apples
1 lb (450 g) sultanas
1 lb (450 g) demerara sugar
2 lb (900 g) onions
2 lb (900 g) tomatoes
2 lb (900 g) plums (stoned)
1½ pints (900 ml/3¾ cups) vinegar
2 oz (50 g) salt
1 teaspoon spice
2 oz (50 g) root ginger (bruised and put in a muslin bag)

Peel, core and chop the apples.

Peel and chop the onions.

Chop the tomatoes and plums.

Put the ingredients in a pan with the sugar, vinegar and spices.

Cook gently for approximately 1½ to 2 hours.

Remove the bag of ginger.

Put in pre-heated airtight jars.

Seal well.

VICTORIA PLUM CHUTNEY

Makes about 6 lbs (2.75 kg)

2 lbs (900 g) Victoria plums
1/2 lb (225 g) onions
1/4 lb (100 g) demerara sugar
1/4 oz (7 g) peppercorns
1 lb (450 g) cooking apples
1/2 lb (225 g) raisins, stoned
1/4 oz (7 g) root ginger
1 1/2 pint (900 ml/3 3/4 cups) malt vinegar
1/2 oz (15 g) salt

Stone and chop the plums

Peel and chop the onions and cooking apples.

Chop the raisins.

Put the root ginger and peppercorn in a muslin bag and tie firmly.

Put the sugar and the vinegar into a saucepan and bring to the boil slowly.

Add the fruit and vegetables.

Put the bag into a pan and cook gently until the mixture thickens to a jam consistency.

Pour into the jars,and seal.

This chutney must be kept for at least three months before use.

ANCHOVY BUTTER

12 anchovies
1 lb (450 g) butter
Bunch of parsley

Wash and bone the anchovies.

Crush to a paste with a mortar.

Boil the parsley and rub it through a sieve.

Mix the anchovies, parsley and butter together.

Make into pats and chill.

MUSHROOM CATSUP (KETCHUP) 2 pints

1 peck mushrooms (4 lbs/1.75 kg)
1 lb (450 g) salt
Liquor to boil
1 oz (25 g) black pepper
1/4 oz (7 g) allspice
1/2 oz (15 g) ginger
2 blades mace

Break a peck of large mushrooms into a deep earthen pan.

Strew three quarters of a pound of salt among them.

Set them into a very cool oven for one night wit a cloth or paper over them.

The following day strain off the liquor, measure 2 pints and boil it for 15 more minutes.

Add the remaining salt, black pepper, allspice, ginger and blades of mace.

Let it boil for 20 minutes

Allow to cool. Put in bottles and seal well.

TRADITIONAL WHITE SAUCE

1 oz (25 g) butter
1 oz (25 g) flour
1/2 pint (300 ml/1 1/4 cups) milk
A bay leaf
1 teaspoon freshly chopped parsley and thyme
1 tablespoon each: onion, turnip, celery, finely chopped
1/2 teaspoon lemon juice
A pinch of cayenne pepper
A pinch of salt

Put the milk in a saucepan with the bay leaf, herbs and vegetables.

Simmer for 4 or 5 minutes.

Strain and reserve the milk stock.

Melt the butter in a saucepan.

Stir in the flour with a wooden spoon.

Cook over a low heat for a few minutes.

Remove from the heat.

Add the milk stock beating in gradually with a wooden spoon.

Return to the heat and continue to beat until the sauce boils.

Simmer for 5 minutes.

Season with cayenne pepper, salt and lemon juice.

If desired a knob of butter can be added to give the sauce a gloss.

Do not boil after the butter is added.

TRADITIONAL PUFF PASTRY

8 oz (225 g) plain flour
6 oz (175 g) butter
Salt
Water to mix
For a richer pastry use equal amounts of butter to flour

Sift the flour.

Cut the butter into small pieces.

Add half the fat to the flour with a pinch of salt and cold water to make a dough.

Knead it quickly and roll until approximately 3/4 inch (19 mm thick).

Add the remaining butter.

Fold and roll again dusting each time with a little flour.

Keep in fridge until ready for use.

Allow to return to room temperature.

TRADITIONAL RICH SHORT CRUST

8 oz (225 g) plain flour
6 oz (175 g) butter
A pinch of salt
1 dessertspoon sugar
Water to mix

Sift the flour.

Break the butter into pieces and work lightly into the flour.

Mix with the salt and sugar.

Add sufficient water to make a firm dough.

Roll out on a floured surface.

TRADITIONAL SUSSEX APPLE PIE Serves 4

8 oz (225 g) shortcrust pastry
1 lb (450 g) cooking apples
4 oz (400 g), sugar
2 oz (50 g) butter
1/2 teaspoon nutmeg
5 fl oz (150 ml/2/3 cup) double cream

Line a pie dish with the shortcrust pastry.

Leave enough pastry for the lid.

Peel and slice the apples and place in the dish.

Cover with the pastry dish.

Seal the edges.

Place in the oven for approximately 30-35 minutes.

Remove from the oven.

Cut of the pastry lid level with the pie dish and turn the lid upside down.

Beat the apples gently whilst in the dish.

Add the sugar, butter, nutmeg and mix with the apples.

Scoop out half the mixture and put in the pastry lid.

Replace the lid upside down so the pie is layered (pie, apple mixture, pie, apple mixture).

Serve with whipped cream on top.

Oven: 400°F/200°C Gas Mark 6

PUMPKIN PIE

Serves 4

1/2 lb (225 g) ripe pumpkin
1/2 lb (225 g) cooking apples
3 ozs (75 g) sugar
4 ozs (100 g) currants
1/2 lb (225 g) puff or shortcrust pasty
2 ozs (50 g) mixed peel
1 teaspoon mixed spice

Peel and seed the pumpkin.

Cut into 1/2 inch cubes.

Peel, core and dice the cooking apples.

Mix the pumpkin, apples, currants, peel and spice together.

Arrange in a buttered pie dish.

Cover with a pastry lid.

Bake in a moderate oven for the first 15 minutes.

Lower the temperature and bake for a further 30 minutes.

Marrow may be used in place of pumpkin.

Oven: 425°F/220°C Gas Mark 7
Reduce to: 350°F/180°C Gas Mark 4

SUSSEX PRUNE PIE

Serves 4

1/2 lb (225 g) dried prunes
2 ozs (50 g) granulated sugar
2 ozs (50 g) caster sugar
2 tablespoons cream
2 eggs separated
1/2 lb (225 g) shortcrust pastry

Soak the prunes overnight.

Stew gently until tender.

Put through the sieve.

Into the fruit pulp beat the granulated sugar, cream and beaten egg yolks.

Line a pie dish with the shortcrust pastry.

Spoon in the mixture.

Bake in a moderate oven for 1/2 hour.

Whip the egg whites until the mixture forms stiff peaks.

Add the caster sugar.

Pile on top of the pudding.

Bake in the oven for a further 5 minutes until crisp.

Oven: 350°F/180°C Gas Mark 4

BLACK EYED SUSAN

Serves 4

A round steamed pudding filled with sweet wine or sherry

8 ozs (225 g) self-raising flour
2 ozs (50 g) lard
1 oz (25 g) butter
1 oz (25 g) brown sugar
A little sherry or homemade wine
2 teaspoons caster sugar
A few currants
A pinch of salt
Milk and water to mix

Sieve the flour and salt.

Rub the fat into the flour.

Add two teaspoonfuls of sugar and the currants.

Mix into a stiff dough with a little milk and water.

Take about a quarter of the mixture and roll into a square.

Put a good nob of butter in the middle, and make into a ball.

Roll out the rest of the paste and gather it round the ball.

Put it all into a greased basin.

Cover and boil for 1½ hours.

Turn out into a dish and cut a round hole out of the centre.

Pour the homemade wine or sherry, mixed with the brown sugar, into the hole.

Replace the cut out piece of the pudding and serve.

ELIZA ACTON'S CHRISTMAS PUDDING

Eliza Acton was born in Battle, Sussex in 1799, and was the daughter of a Hastings brewer. Her comprehensive cookery book 'Modern cooking for Private Families' was first published in 1845 and was the forerunner to Mrs Beeton's more famous book of the 1860s.

The book is full of the best plain English dishes. However, it was written at a time when more varied food were becoming available - the emergence of an efficient railway network meant better distribution, especially of imported produce - which was soon to widen the British appetite.

3 oz (75 g) flour
3 oz (75 g) breadcrumbs
6 oz (175 g) stoned raisins
6 oz (175 g) currants
6 oz (175 g) suet
4 oz (100 g) apples minced
5 oz (150 g) sugar
2 oz (50 g) candied peel
1/2 teaspoon mixed mace and nutmeg
Salt
Small glass brandy
3 eggs

To three ounces of flour and the same weight of fine, lightly grated bread-crumbs, add six of beef kidney-suet, chopped small, six of raisins, weighed after they are stoned, six of well-cleaned currants, four ounces of minced apples, five of sugar, two of candied orange-rind, lay a teaspoonful of nutmeg, mixed with pounded mace, a very little salt, a small glass of brandy and tree whole eggs. Mix and beat these ingredients well together, tie them tightly in a thickly floured cloth and boil them for three hours and a half.

SUSSEX POND PUDDING

Serves 4

This delicious pudding that looks like a huge apple dumpling, but has a buttery lemon pond inside, was traditionally eaten on Palm Sunday.

8 oz (225 g) self-raising flour
1/4 teaspoon salt
4 oz (100 g) shredded suet
4 fl ozs (6 tablespoons/1/2 cup) iced water
4 ozs (100 g) butter, diced
4 ozs (100 g) brown sugar
1 large lemon

Sift the flour and salt into a bowl.

Add the shredded suet and mix lightly with a fork.

Make a well in the centre and add the water, a little at a time, to make a soft dough.

Knead the dough lightly on a floured surface until it is free of cracks.

Roll it out to a thickened of about 1/4 inch.

Cut a quarter segment from the dough and set it aside for the lid.

Use the remaining dough to line a well-buttered pudding basin (1 1/2 pts).

Put half the diced butter in the bottom of the basin.

Prick the lemon all over with a skewer and sit it upright in the butter.

Cover with the remaining butter and the sugar.

Roll out the reserved dough for a lid.

Dampen the edges and press it gently into place.

Cover the basin with greaseproof paper and foil.

Stand the basin in a saucepan and pour in the boiling water to come to a third of the way up the sides.

Cover the pan tightly and simmer for $3^{1/2}$ hours - topping up with water from time to time and never allowing it to go off the boil.

Rest the pudding for a moment or two before turning out onto a deep plate.

Make sure each serving includes a slice of lemon.

PLUM DUFF

Serves 3-4

This is an early 19th century recipe. In Sussex Plum Duff is also known as Hunt Pudding. Duff is a colloquialism for dough. Traditionally puddings were steamed directly in the cloth..

4 oz (100 g) plain flour
1 teaspoon baking powder
1 oz (25 g) caster sugar
2 oz (50 g) chopped suet
3 oz (75 g) raisins
1/2 teaspoon mixed spice
1/4 pint (150 ml/2/3 cup) milk
2 tablespoons redcurrant jelly

Sift the flour and baking powder together.

Add the sugar, suet, raisins and spice.

Mix well.

Pour in the milk and mix to a stiff consistency.

Flour a cloth (large enough to wrap the pudding in).

Place pudding on the cloth, allow a little space on top, and tie ends securely.

Boil for $2^{1/2}$ hours.

Before serving melt redcurrant jelly and pour over the pudding.

BLACK CAP PUDDING

Serves 5-6

Black Cap is a village near Lewes, East Sussex.

5 oz (150 g) flour
2 eggs
1/2 **pint (300 ml/1$^{1/4}$ cups) milk**
1 oz (25 g) sugar
1/4 **teaspoon salt**
4 oz (100 g) raisins or currants

Sieve the flour.

Mix in the eggs to make a batter by pouring the milk in slowly and beating well.

Grease the pudding basin.

Cover the bottom with the raisins or currants.

Pour the batter into the basin.

Cover with a cloth and tie down securely and steam for 1$^{1/2}$ hours.

CHICHESTER PIE

Serves 3-4

A cinnamon flavoured custard pudding

1/2 **pint (300 ml/1$^{1/4}$ cups) milk**
2 ozs ('50 g) sugar
3 eggs (separated)
3 ozs (75 g) fresh white breadcrumbs
Cinnamon to flavour

Warm the milk to blood heat.

Pour over the beaten egg yolks

Mix in the sugar.

Beat the egg whites until stiff.

Add the breadcrumbs to the milk mixture.

Stir in the cinnamon to taste.

Fold in the egg whites but only sufficiently to give a marbled effect.

Pour in the mixture into a greased 1 pint dish.

Stand the dish in a pan of hot water.

Bake in the oven for 30-40 minutes until the custard is set.

Oven: 350°F/180°C Gas Mark 4

CURD CHEESECAKE

This is an old recipe recorded by Mary Anne Woodman of Stanmer in 1833, and entitled 'My Mother's Curd Cheesecake'.

2 pints (1.15 litres/5 cups) curd cheese
Six egg yolks
Teaspoonful grated nutmeg
1/2 lb (225 g) sugar
1/4 lb (100 g) butter
1 lb (450 g) currants
Orange flower water
(A little fresh orange juice could be used)
Puff paste (puff pastry)

Beat the curd cheese in a mortar as fine as butter.

Put to it the yolks of six eggs and some grated nutmeg, the sugar and butter melted without water. Mix all together.

Then put in the currants and a little orange flower water or orange juice.

Put a puff paste at the bottom of your pans and if you please leave in half the whites of your eggs.

PIPPIN DESSERT

Serves 4

The Pippin apple is believed to originate from Arundel, Sussex and has been popular since Tudor times as both a dessert apple and for cider making.

3 Pippin apples
2 eggs
1/2 pint (300 ml/1 1/4 cups) single cream
2 oz (50 g) caster sugar
2 oz (50 g) breadcrumbs
1/2 teaspoon nutmeg
2-3 oz (50-75 g) butter

Peel, core and slice the apples.

Beat the eggs with the cream. Add the sugar, breadcrumbs and nutmeg.

Melt the butter in a saucepan.

Cook the apples gently in the butter.

Do not allow them to break up.

Pour the cream mixture over the apples, stirring gently.

Allow to thicken in the pan.

Remove from the pan and place on a serving dish.

Sprinkle with sugar and serve

PIPPIN TARTS

Makes 24

1 lb (450 g) puff pastry
6 Pippin apples
6 tomatoes
4 oz (100 g) sugar
5 tablespoons single cream

Make up the pastry (see recipe for Traditional Puff Pastry).

Allow to rest.

Roll out on a floured surface.

Cut individual 3 inch (7.5 cm) rounds.

Grease the patty tins.

Line with the pastry rounds.

Peel, core and slice the apples.

Skin and cut up the tomatoes.

Put the apple and tomatoes in a pan.

Add sugar and simmer until tender.

Stir in the cream and put the mixture into tart cases.

Cover with pastry lid. Seal the edges.

Cook for 25-30 minutes.

Oven: 375°F/190°C Gas Mark 5

TOMATOES FOR DESSERT

Serves 4

In the early to mid 19th century, vegetables which are more commonly used today in salads, such as lettuce, tomatoes and cucumber, were mainly served cooked - and in some interesting ways.

1 lb (450 g) tomatoes
1 lb (450 g) sugar
2 lemons - grated peel and juice
1/4 pint (150 ml/2/3 cup) water

Pour boiling water over the tomatoes.

Skin and peel off the skins.

Make a syrup by boiling the water and sugar until the sugar dissolves.

Add the tomatoes.

Continue to cook, simmering, and add the peel of the lemons, grated finely.

Add lemon juice.

Continue to cook until the fruit is clear.

Remove the fruit and continue to boil the syrup until thick.

Leave to cool.

Put the fruit in a jar.

Pass the syrup through a sieve and pour over the fruit.

Seal the jar tightly.

(It may be well to look at it a few weeks after it is stored).

SUSSEX LEMONY DELIGHT

Serves 4

A refreshing dessert.

3 lemons
1 pint (600 ml/2 1/2 cups) water
7 oz (200 g) sugar
1 1/2 oz (40 g) cornflour
3 egg whites

Bring 3/4 pint (450 ml/2 cups) of water to the boil in a saucepan.

Meanwhile mix the cornflour with the remaining water to a smooth paste.

Pour boiling water over the cornflour and mix well.

Return to the pan and boil, stirring continuously, until thickened.

Stir in the sugar and allow to cool.

Grate the rind of the lemons and squeeze the juice.

Beat the egg whites until stiff.

Add the lemon juice and fold in the egg whites into the cornflour mixture.

Pour into a mould or serving dish and leave to set.

RHUBARB MERINGUE

Serves 4

$1^{1/2}$ lb (675 g) young rhubarb
10 oz (275 g) granulated sugar
3 eggs
A little water

Wash and cut the rhubarb into equal lengths.

Put in a pan with 8 oz (225 g) of the sugar and a little water (2-3 tablespoons).

Cook very gently until the fruit is tender and the juice is thickened.

Allow to cool.

Separate the egg whites from the yolks.

Whisk the egg whites until stiff.

Fold in the remaining sugar.

Place the fruit in a pie dish.

Cover well with the egg white mixture.

Cook in a moderate oven for approximately 15 minutes or until the meringue top has browned.

Oven: 160°C/325°F Gas Mark 3

TIPSY SUSSEX SQUIRE

Serves 8

This dish from Michelham Priory, is best made a day prior to serving.

1 plain spoinge (to fit large serving dish)
8 oz (225 g) ratafia biscuits
4 dessertspoons of different jams e.g. strawberry, raspberry, blackcurrant, apricot
1 dessertspoon marmalade
2-3 tablespoons (or to taste) brandy
2-3 tablespoons (or to taste) sherry
1 oz (25 g) chopped almonds

For the custard:
6 eggs
3 oz (75 g) caster sugar
1½ pints (900 ml/3¾ cups) milk

Soak ratafia biscuits in brandy.

Line the dish with biscuits.

Cut the sponge in half. Cut the bottom half in 5 slices and spread each slice with different jam and marmalade.

Add to the dish jam side up.

Pour sherry and brandy over the sponge.

Sprinkle with the chopped almonds.

Place the remaining half of the sponge on top as a cover.

To make the custard:

Blend together the egg yolks with the sugar in a bowl.

Put the milk in a pan and warm over a low heat.

Pour the milk over the egg mixture.

Return to the pan and cook, stirring continuously. Do not allow to simmer.

When thickened, pour over the sponge and leave to set.

MILK CHOCOLATE NUT CAKE WITH CHOCOLATE GLAZE

8 oz (225 g) self-raising flour
6 oz (175 g) butter or margarine
2 eggs
4 oz (100 g) milk chocolate
2 oz (50 g) almonds
4 oz (100 g) caster sugar
1/4 pint (150 ml/2/3 cup) milk

For the chocolate glaze:
4 oz (100 g) milk chocolate
8 oz (225 g) icing sugar
1/4 teaspoon vanilla essence
1 oz (25 g) almonds
A little water to mix

Cream the butter and sugar together.

Beat the eggs, and add them gradually to the mixture.

Blanch and chop the almonds.

Fold them into the mixture with the flour.

Add the milk and mix to a smooth batter.

Put into greased cake tin.

Bake in a moderate oven for approximately 1 1/2 hours.

To make the chocolate glaze:

Grate the chocolate and melt in a bowl standing in a saucepan of hot water.

When melted beat until smooth.

Sieve the icing sugar.

Stir in the melted chocolate and vanilla essence

Add enough cold water to mix to a smooth coating cream.

Pour the glaze over the chocolate cake, and smooth with a knife dipped in hot water.

Blanch and split the almonds.

Use to decorate the top of the cake.

Oven: 350°F/180°C Gas Mark 4

SUSSEX BLACK CAKE

6 oz (175 g) butter
1/2 cup (4 fl oz/6 tablespoons) tepid milk
3 eggs
1/2 teaspoon baking powder
8 oz (225 g) sieved plain flour
4 oz (100 g) black treacle
4 oz (100 g) sugar
8 oz (225 g) dried mixed fruit

Cream the fat and sugar.

Beat in the black treacle, then the eggs, one at the time.

Add the milk, fruit, flour and baking powder.

Grease an 8 inch round cake tin.

Pour in the mixture.

Bake in a slow oven for 2 1/2 hours or until cooked.

Oven: 325°F/160°C Gas Mark 3

LARDY JOHNS

Makes 9 squares

4 ozs (100 g) self-raising flour
2 ozs (50 g) lard
2 teaspoon caster sugar
2 ozs (50 g) currants
Water to mix

Rub flour and lard together.

Add the sugar and currants.

Mix with a little water to make a stiff paste.

Roll out and cut into 2 inch squares.

Put on a greased baking sheet.

Bake for 20 minutes, turning to brown on the other side if necessary.

Oven: 350°F/180°C Gas Mark 4

BRIGHTON ROCKS

Makes 18

4 ozs (100 g) butter or margarine
2 eggs
2 ozs (50 g) ground almonds
2 ozs (50 g) currants
4 ozs (100 g) caster sugar
8 ozs (225 g) plain flour
1 beaten egg (optional)

Cream the butter until soft, then beat in the eggs.

Fold in the almonds, currants, sugar and sifted flour.

Work the mixture until smooth.

Shape into buns.

Set on a greased baking tray.

Brush with beaten egg and bake in a hot oven for 10 minutes.

Oven: 425°F/220°C Gas Mark 7

SUSSEX PLUM HEAVIES

Makes 24

1 lb (450 g) flour
2 ozs (50 g) lard
2 ozs (50 g) margarine
4 ozs (100 g) raisins
1 oz (25 g) caster sugar
4 teaspoons baking powder
1 teacupful milk
Juice of 1/2 lemon

Add the lemon juice to the cup of milk to sour.

Stone the raisins and halve.

Sift the flour and baking powder.

Rub the fat into the flour.

Add the raisins and sugar.

Mix with the milk to a stiff dough.

Roll out to an inch in thickness, and cut into rounds.

Brush over with a little soured milk.

Sprinkle with caster sugar.

Bake in a fairly hot oven.

Best eaten while hot.

Note: 4 ozs currants may be substituted for the raisins.

Oven: 400°F/200°C Gas Mark 6

OATY SLICES

Makes 24

14 oz (400 g) rolled oats
8 oz (225 g) margarine or softened butter
8 oz (225 g) soft brown sugar
2 tablespoons thick marmalade
2 tablespoons clear honey

Cream the margarine or butter with the sugar.

Add the honey and marmalade.

Mix well.

Add the oats and combine the ingredients thoroughly.

Grease a baking tin.

Pour in the mixture.

Bake for 30-35 minutes.

Allow to cool on the tin.

Cut into finger-sized slices to serve.

Note: These slices will keep well in an airtight container.

Oven: 325°F/160°C Gas Mark 3